CAPOEIRA
AN EXERCISE OF THE SOUL

CAPOEIRA
AN EXERCISE OF THE SOUL

Text by C. DANIEL DAWSON

This book is a publication of
Diasporic Africa Press
NEW YORK | WWW.DAFRICAPRESS.COM
Copyright @ Diasporic Africa Press 2020

All rights reserved. No part of this publication may be reproduced or distributed in any form or by any means, or stored in a database or retrieval system, without the prior written permission of the publisher.

Library of Congress Control Number: 2016952367

ISBN-13 978-1-937306-46-5 (pbk.: alk paper)
ISBN-13 978-1-937306-47-2 (ebook)

Diasporic Africa Press uses environmentally friendly book materials, including recycled text paper that is composed of at least 30 percent post-consumer waste, whenever possible.

Printed in the United States of America on acid-free paper.

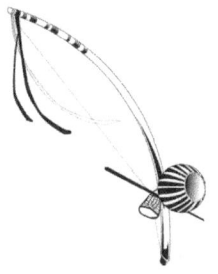

The Atlantic slave trade, sometimes known as the Middle Passage, caused havoc on the cultures and political states of Africa and led to the forced migration of millions of Africans to the Americas. The Africans could not bring their material cultures and artifacts, but most important, they brought their histories and cultures—philosophies, languages, political structures, and religious and artistic expressions.

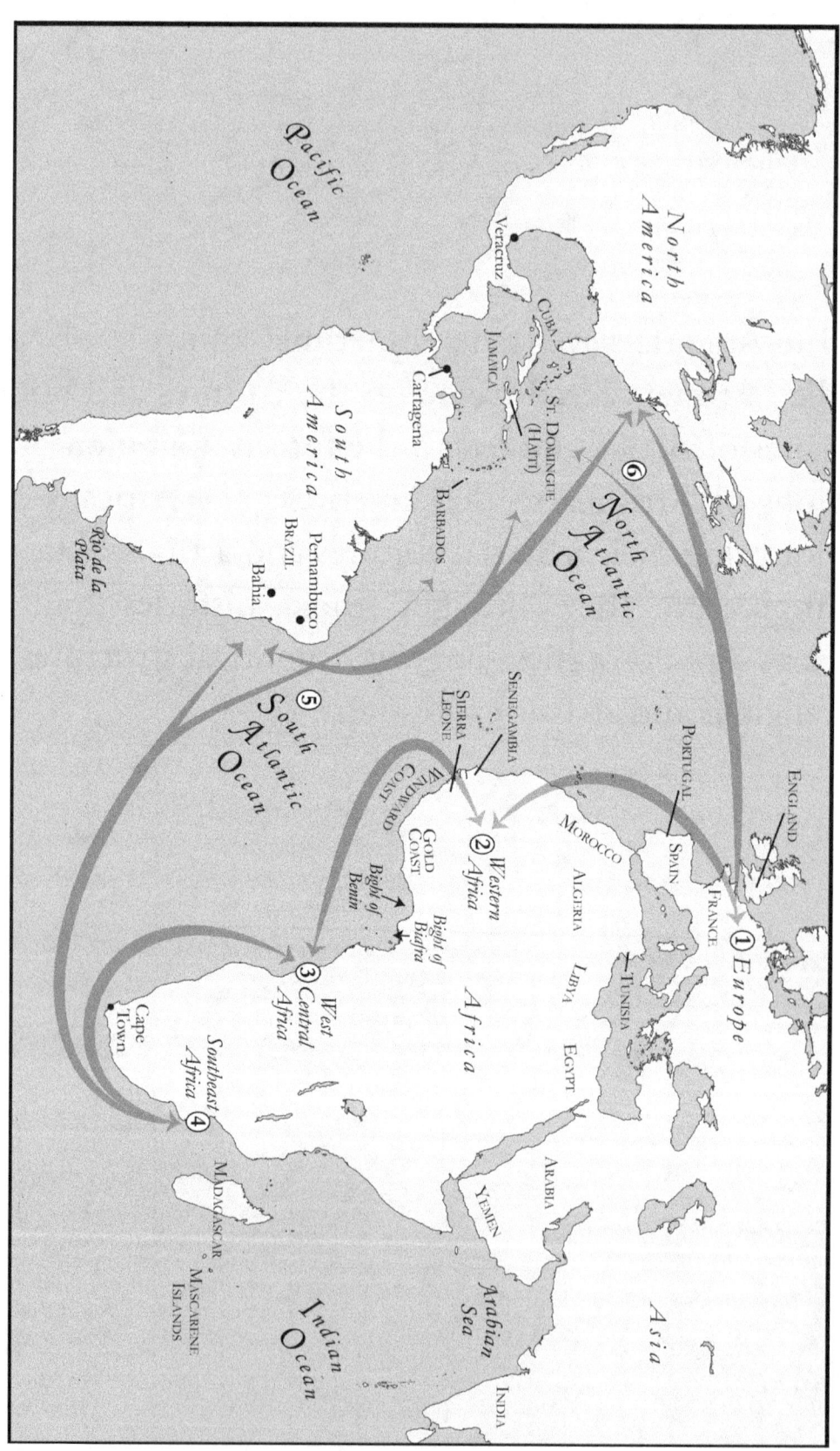

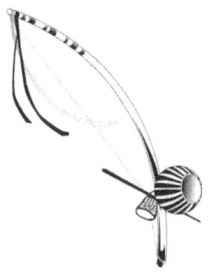

Hundreds of societies were established throughout the Americas by Africans who had freed themselves. These societies were called *maroons* in the United States, *palenques* in the Spanish-speaking countries, and *quilombos* or *mocambos* in Brazil. The most famous *mocambo* was the Quilombo dos Palmares, which existed for almost one hundred years as an independent nation made up of Africans, indigenous peoples, and poor whites. Many of these societies had their own system of self-defense or martial arts which, not surprisingly, had their origins in Africa.

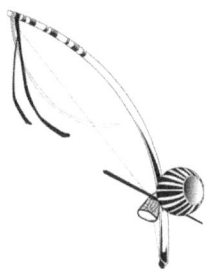

Africans practiced a variety of martial arts. In the past, these techniques were usually practiced by young male warriors, but in a few cases like the ancient Kingdom of Dahomey and Angola women were also warriors. Higher, more sacred techniques were part of special knowledge that was guarded by a council of elders and taught only after strenuous initiations into warrior societies. From the top of northern Africa to the bottom of southern Africa there were and still are hundreds of fighting styles that emphasized skill, technique, and intelligence over brute force. Several scholars, including T. J. Desch-Obi, Rick Johnson, Patrick Gorham/Lanfia Toure, and Mestre Cobra Mansa, have dutifully documented the historical connection between Africa and the Americas. One of the martial arts that sprang from this connection, *capoeira angola,* is still played in Brazil and around the world today.

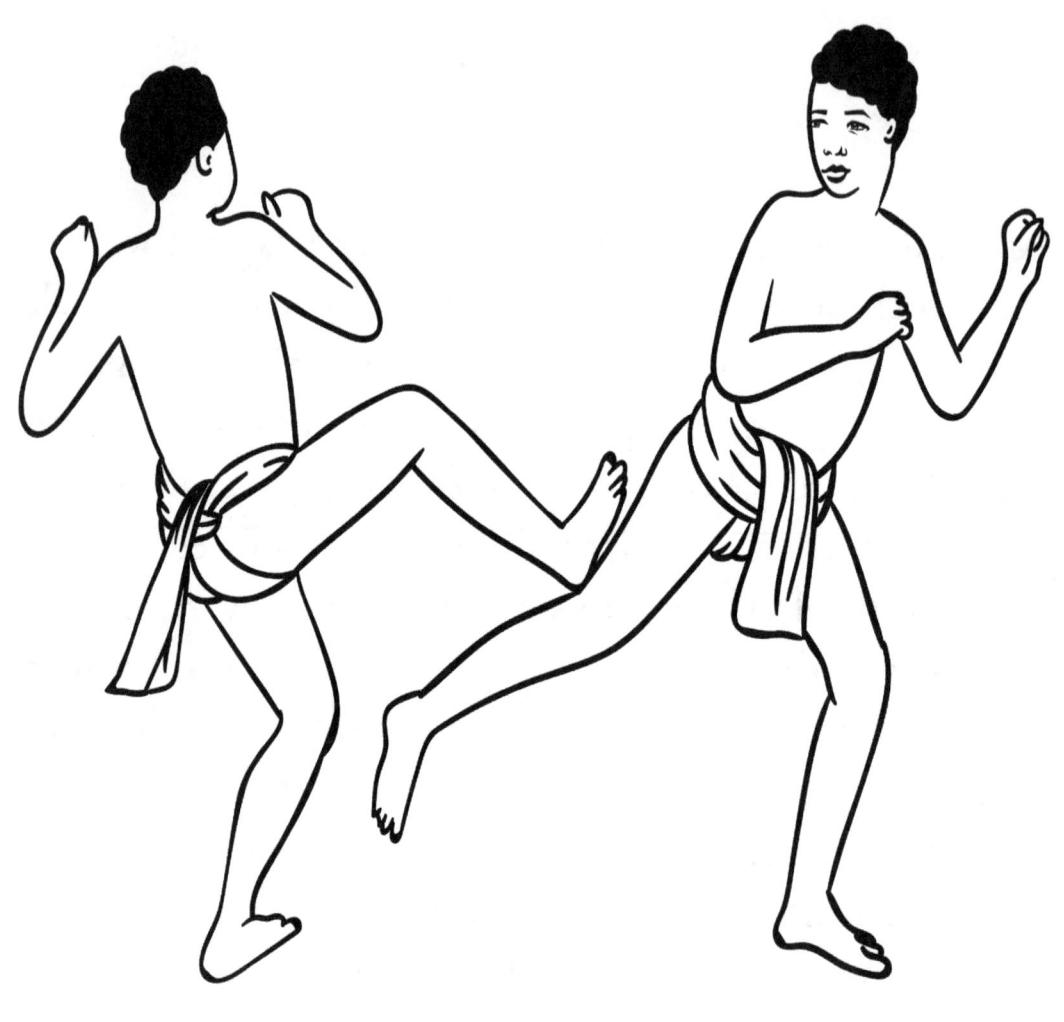

Diamango style of martial arts and kickboxing in Madagascar.

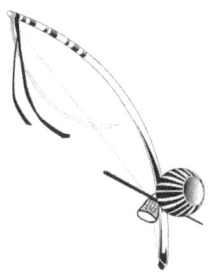

As its name suggests, the search for the origins of *capoeira angola* should start in Angola. Albano de Neves e Souza of Angola wrote in an old letter that "N'golo *is* capoeira." Albano described *n'golo* as an acrobatic zebra dance performed by young males of the Mucope people of Angola. The dance had an aspect of competition: The man chosen as the best dancer was permitted to select a wife without having to pay the bride's family a marriage fee. The late Vincente Pastinha, the famous *capoeira angola* master of Brazil, stated that his own teacher, a man from Angola named Benedito, told him that *capoeira* was developed from the *n'golo* dance. Other references suggest different origins, although still from the same area in Central Africa.

Wagenia wrestlers from the Democratic Republic of Congo, in Central Africa

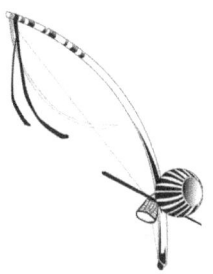

Mário Barcelos wrote in *Aruanda,* "Next to the Cambindas, there existed another people that played capoeira. They were the Mazingas, of the Congo, that were the eternal adversaries of the Cambindas in that art." Angola has other martial arts such as *njinga, basula,* and *gabetula.* These are considered forms that are similar to *capoeira angola* and helped create it. Add all the sources together: the *n'golo* dance, the art of the Mazinga and the Cambinda, the other martial dances of Angola, and you come to the general conclusion that *capoeira angola* began in Central Africa and traveled to Brazil as an already formed art, a fusion of the elements of dance, music, theater, and ritual. *Capoeira* may have evolved once it arrived in Brazil, but its origin is African.

Ladja fighting sytle in Martinique.

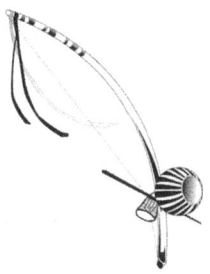

Capoeira traveled with the Atlantic slave trade to Brazil, where it became an outlaw art. Legend has it that *capoeira* was used by Africans to fight slavery and oppression in the Portuguese colonial society. During the time of slavery the practice of *capoeira* was punishable by death. But the Brazilian government was finally forced to recognize the fighting skills of *capoeiristas,* as practitioners are called; in their war with Paraguay in the 1860s the *capoeiristas* served as front-line troops. More than 65,000 African-Brazilians died in that war.

Juego de Mani (game of war) martial arts and dance in Cuba with Kongo and Angola roots.

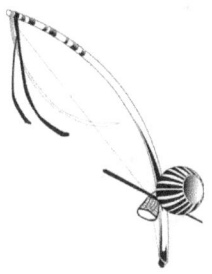

After the abolition of slavery in 1888 *capoeira* continued as an outlaw art form, but by then it had become a part of Brazilian society. It was practiced by Africans, Europeans, and those of mixed heritage, and in a few cases by those of the upper classes. At this time, *capoeira* was also used as an intimidation tactic. Roving bands of *capoeristas* were employed by politicians to intimidate opponents and by businessmen to put the competition out of business. In addition, it was the art of the hustlers and petty thieves who hung out in the streets of Salvador, Bahia, and Rio de Janeiro; their favorite weapon was a straight razor or a dagger.

Capoeira scene in the nineteenth century, associating it with criminal behavior.

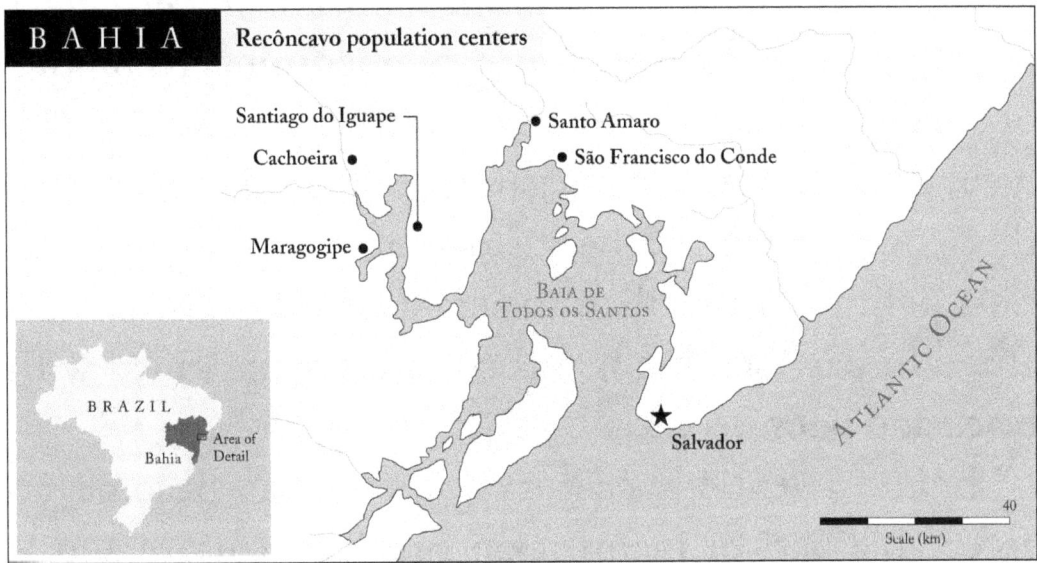

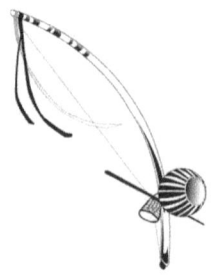

Even today the legacy of associating *capoeira* with crime can be found in the *Novo Michaelis Illustrated Dictionary* of 1983, which defines *capoeira* as a "criminal technique of sudden, violent assault, characterized by agile movement of the body." The negative view of *capoeira* is further complicated by the history of racial conflict and class politics in Brazilian society. *Capoeira* was marginalized in part because it was commonly identified with black and poor people.

In the twentieth century *capoeira* has become an acceptable part of mainstream Brazilian culture and is acknowledged as a national sport. The *jogo-de-capoeira*, or play of *capoeira*, takes place at a *roda* (pronounced HO-da), a *capoeira* party at which *capoeiristas* gather to play. The players and onlookers form a circle, also called a *roda*. At the "top" of the circle is an ensemble of musicians and singers, known as the *bateria*.

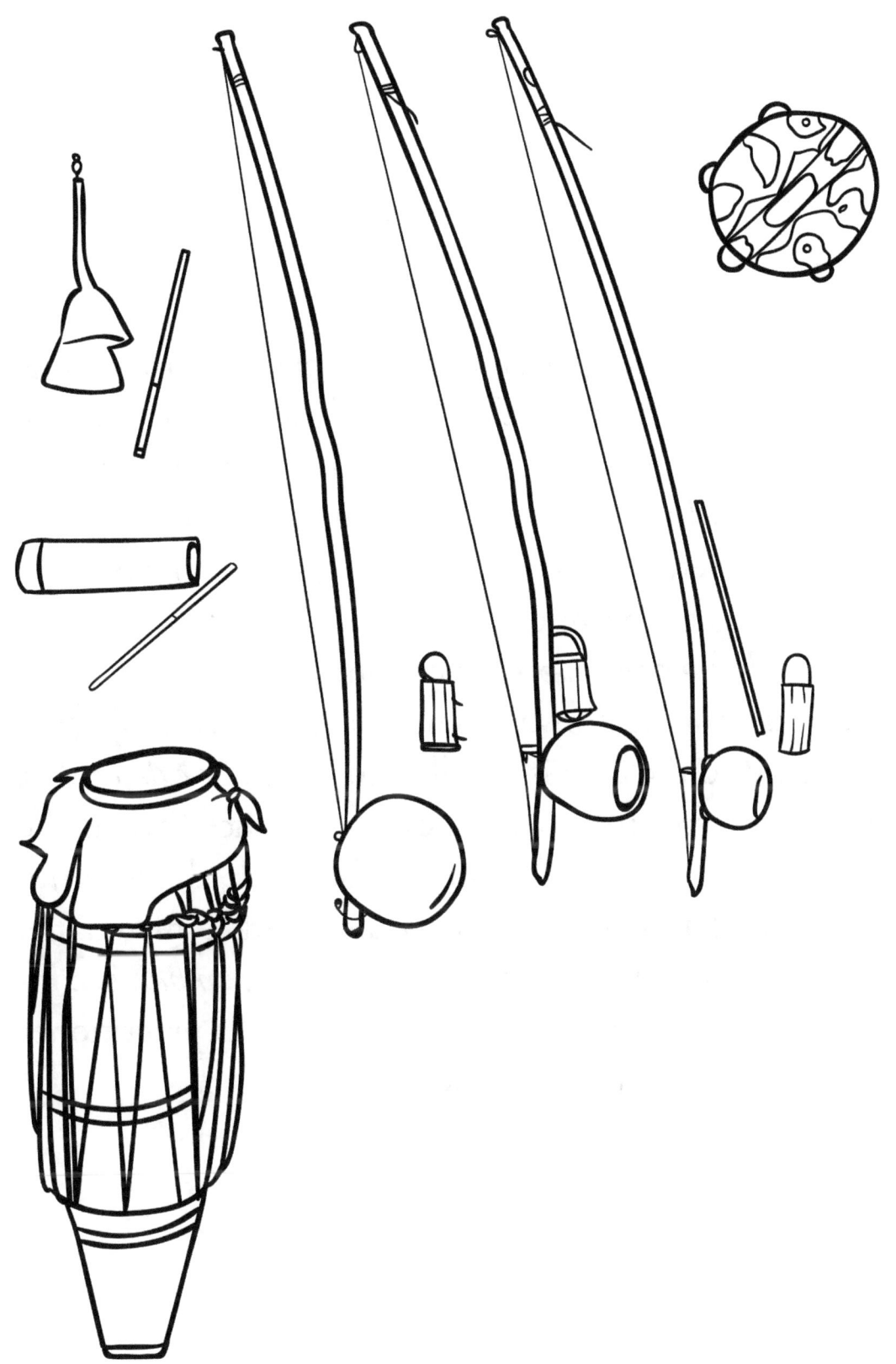

Capoeira instruments.

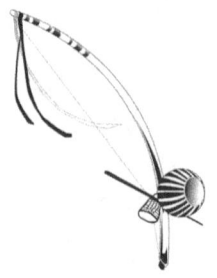

Capoeira is rarely played without music. Music is one of the most important elements of the art, creating the atmosphere in which *capoeira* is most beautifully expressed. Music inspires the *capoeiristas* to more intense levels of interaction and is also used to calm them down when the game becomes too heated.

    The *berimbau,* a bow with one string, is the most important musical instrument associated with *capoeira*. Attached to the bow is a hollowed gourd or *cabaça* that acts as a resonator box. Tones are produced when the bowstring is struck by a thin flexible stick, the *baqueta.* The hand that holds the *baqueta* also holds a small rattle, or *caxixi.* With its hypnotic sound, the *berimbau* is considered "the soul of *capoeira*" by scholar-practitioner Mester Acordeon (Bira Almeida).

Playing berimbau and mbira, often called a "thumb piano," 1826.

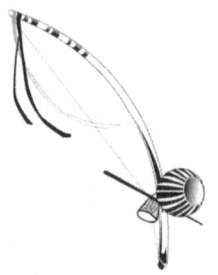

In traditional *capoeira angola* schools, the musicians are placed in a particular order. One sees, from left to right: a *ganza* or *reco-reco,* a notched length of bamboo or a notched gourd played by scraping with a thin stick; an *agogo,* a double-headed bell struck with a stick or thin metal rod; a *pandeiro,* a tambourine; a *berimbau-gunga,* the *berimbau* with the largest gourd, which maintains the rhythm; a *berimbau-centro,* a *berimbau* with a mid-sized gourd, which also maintains the rhythm; a *berimbau-viola,* the smallest *berimbau,* which "speaks," that is, improvises the rhythms; a second *pandeiro*; and an *atabaque,* a drum played with the hands, similar to a conga drum. The dominant instruments are the three *berimbaus*; no other instrument should be played louder than they are. The types and use of songs also have an established order. In all, music is one of the most enriching aspects of *capoeira*.

Mestre João Grande playing the pandeiro, 1988.

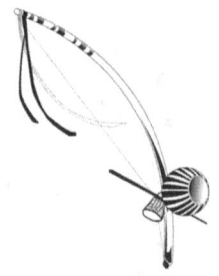

The ritual of *capoeira* begins when two players enter the circle and kneel at the foot of the *berimbaus*. Still kneeling, one player sings a ritual song of commencement accompanied by the musicians. If his opponent does not respond with a song of his own, he begins a second song, a song for going out to play. The song is then passed on to one of the musicians, who continues singing it as the *joga-de-capoeira* begins.

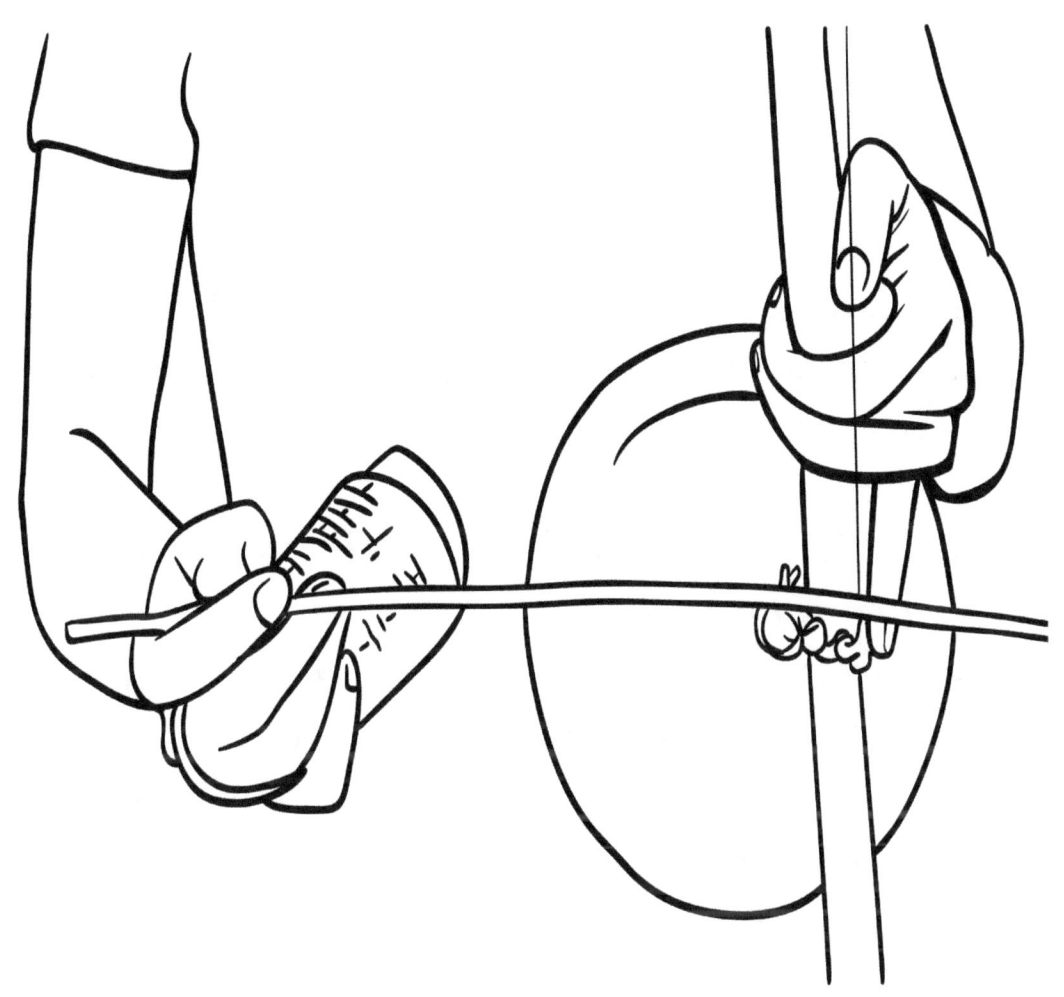

Capoeirista playing the berimbau.

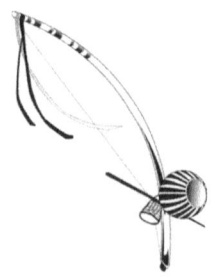

A *capoeira* game is characterized by dynamic movements: cartwheels, handstands, spinning kicks, and spontaneous acrobatics. At its highest level, *capoeira* is considered an improvisational conversation between two bodies. This sensibility is very similar to a jazz performance. As *capoeira* scholar Kenneth Dossar writes in the *Afro-Hispanic Review*:

The object of the game is for the *capoeiristas* to use finesse, guile, and technique to maneuver one another into a defenseless position, rendering them open to a blow, kick, or sweep. Only one's hands, head, and feet are allowed to touch the floor. Being swept and landing on one's bottom disqualifies a player. In general, there is no contact from strikes. An implied strike is more admired...

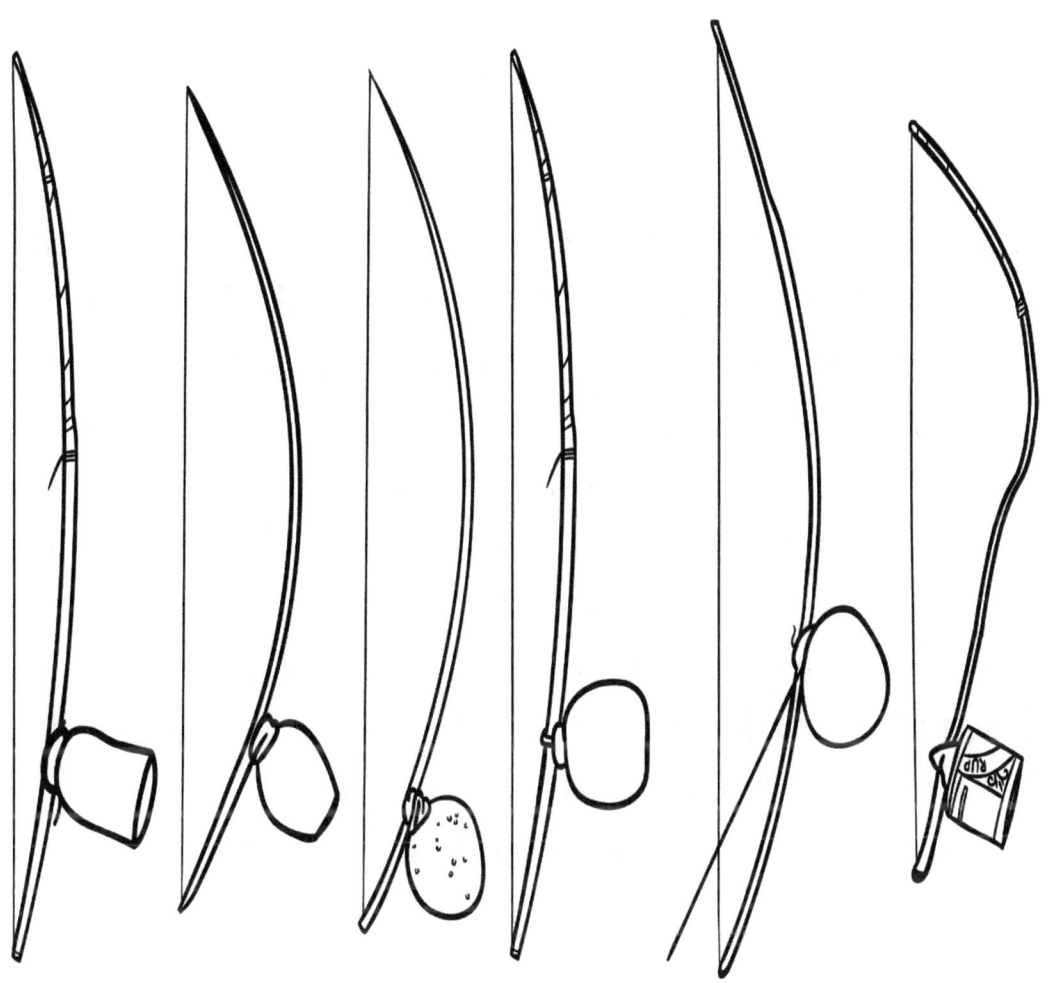

South African musical bows.

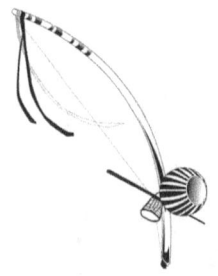

Capoeira utilizes few offensive hand techniques. Some attribute this to the belief that enslaved Africans had to fight with their hands in chains and therefore emphasized foot and leg techniques. It is more likely, however, that the absence of hand techniques is based on an ancient Kongo tradition in which hands should be used for good work, that is, creative activities, whereas feet should be used for bad work, that is, punishment and destruction. Bakongo scholar Dr. K. Kia Bunseki Fu-Kiau recalls a relevant proverb in Kikongo, *Mooko mu tunga, malu mu diatikisa* (Hands are to build, feet are to destroy).

Kongolese man playing the berimbau in Rio de Janeiro, Brazil, 1826.

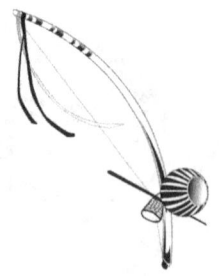

African practices tend not to separate parts of the culture into isolated and differentiated activities. *Capoeira* is no exception. Scholar Dr. Alejandro Frigerio writes, "*Capoeira*... is a multiform phenomenon: it is dance, fight, game, ritual and musical performance. It is a person's way of defense, and it is also a form of entertainment." It is based on African and African-Brazilian values. Dr. Frigerio identifies six elements intrinsic to modern *capoeira angola: malicia,* complementation, beautiful movement, slow rhythm, ritual, and theatrical aspects.

Capoeira scene in Brazil, 1835.

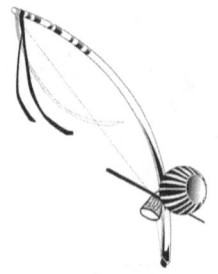

Malicia is the art of being tricky or deceptive. In African America it is called "tricknology" or "oky doke." One aspect of *malicia* is to look vulnerable until the opponent attacks, then gracefully defend or counter-attack. One should play closed, while appearing open.

Mestres João Grande and Cobra Mansa playing capoeira in New York City, 1992.

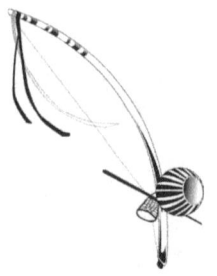

When playing *capoeira* one plays *with*, not *against*, the opponent; this has been described as complementation. It is similar to a "cutting session" in jazz in which the musicians try to outplay each other, the ultimate goal being the creation of beautiful music. Good *capoeira angola* is created with a flowing movement that produces the most creative interaction possible, limited only by the skills of the players.

African-based fighting style in Venezuela, 1874.

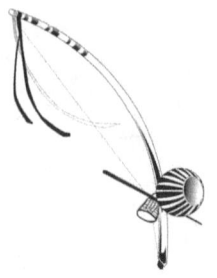

It is not enough merely to "beat" the opponent; one must prove superior skill by displaying it with style, or beautiful movement. This is true for almost all African-descended participation in sports including soccer, basketball, and boxing. Many sports commentators have misunderstood the black athlete and accused him of "showboating" or "hot-dogging," when in reality the athlete was manifesting an African aesthetic concerning beautiful movement.

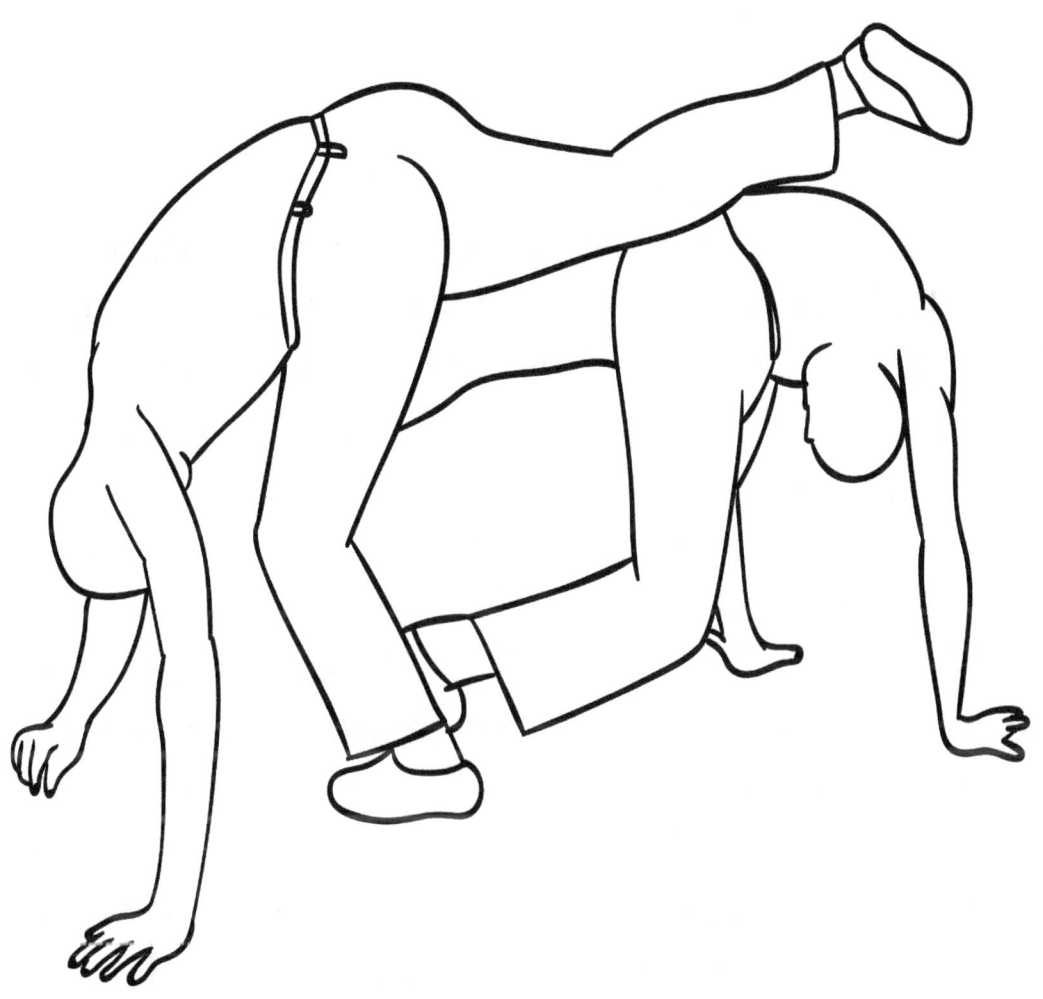

Mestres João Grande and João Pequeno, 1980.

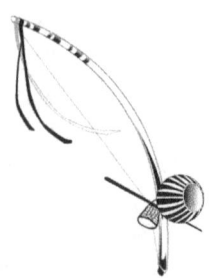

The movement of *capoeira angola* generally has a slow and deliberate rhythm. As in many Chinese and Indian martial arts systems, if one can execute a movement slowly and perfectly, one can also execute it quickly and effectively. *Capoeira angola* is a sophisticated ritual. If a player displays ignorance of these traditional, unwritten rules, he is considered an inferior player.

The *jogo* or play is performed before a group of spectators. Viewers should be entertained by the skill, deception, and humor of the play.

None have exhibited these six elements more skillfully than the two most famous modem masters, Mestre Bimba and Mestre Pastinha, who shaped the development of modern *capoeira.*

Mestre Bimba playing the berimbau.

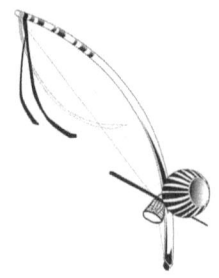

Mestre Bimba (1899-1979) was born Manoel dos Reis Machado in the Brotas section of Salvador. He was first taught to fight by his father, a champion *batuque* fighter. *Batuque* was an African-based martial dance also found in Brazil and similar to *capoeira*. At the age of twelve, Bimba was introduced to *capoeira* by Bentinho (Nozinho Bento), an African from Angola who worked as a ship's captain for the Navigation Company of Bahia. Having learned it, Bimba became its great innovator. He combined elements of *batuque, capoeira,* and free-style fighting to create what he called *capoeira regional: a luta biana* (a Bahia fight). Bimba, a great singer, was also the best fighter of his time, a champion who faced all challengers and never lost a match. A large powerful man, he liked to fight, so it is not surprising that *capoeira regional* stressed the fighting aspect and deemphasized the African cultural elements, which Bimba viewed as unnecessary.

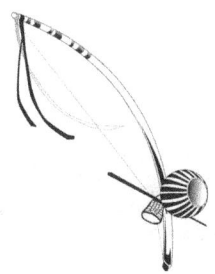

Bimba opened a public academy in 1927. In 1937 it became the first *capoeira* academy to be registered with the Brazilian government. But Brazilians could attend the academy only if they had a job or were in school. These restrictions prevented enrollment by almost all African-Brazilians. Bimba wanted to change the image of *capoeira* by encouraging middle- and upper-class Brazilians to participate in it. Ultimately, embraced by the most influential classes of society, declared legitimate by government officials, and featured in numerous newspaper articles, *capoeira regional* became famous throughout the country.

Mestre Bimba photographed in the newspaper A Tarde, headlined, "It's Not Easy to Catch a Capoeirista."

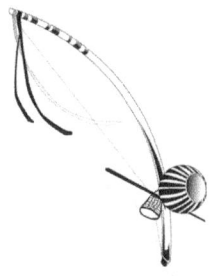

Despite the success of *capoeira regional,* Bimba did not receive much financial gain. He died broke and bitter. *Capoeira regional* was the most popular *capoeira* style in Brazil, but it no longer contained its deep cultural roots. Meanwhile, *capoeira regional* was changed even more by Bimba's students after his death.

Mestre Bimba (right) singing with other capoeiristas.

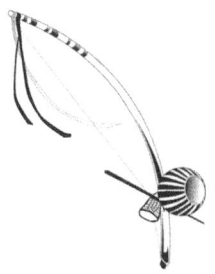

The other legendary modern *capoerista* was Mestre Pastinha (1889-1981). Born Vincente Ferreira Pastinha on April 5, 1889, he played *capoeira* for more than eighty years. His father was a Spaniard, his mother, an African. Like Bimba, he was taught *capoeira* by an African from Angola, Mestre Benedito. Benedito had seen the ten-year-old Pastinha, who was very small in stature, being beaten by a stronger boy. Afterward, he offered to teach Pastinha something very valuable. Benedito was, of course, talking about *capoeira angola,* or *n'golo* as he also called it. Pastinha was a brilliant *capoeirista* whose game was characterized by agility, quickness, and intelligence.

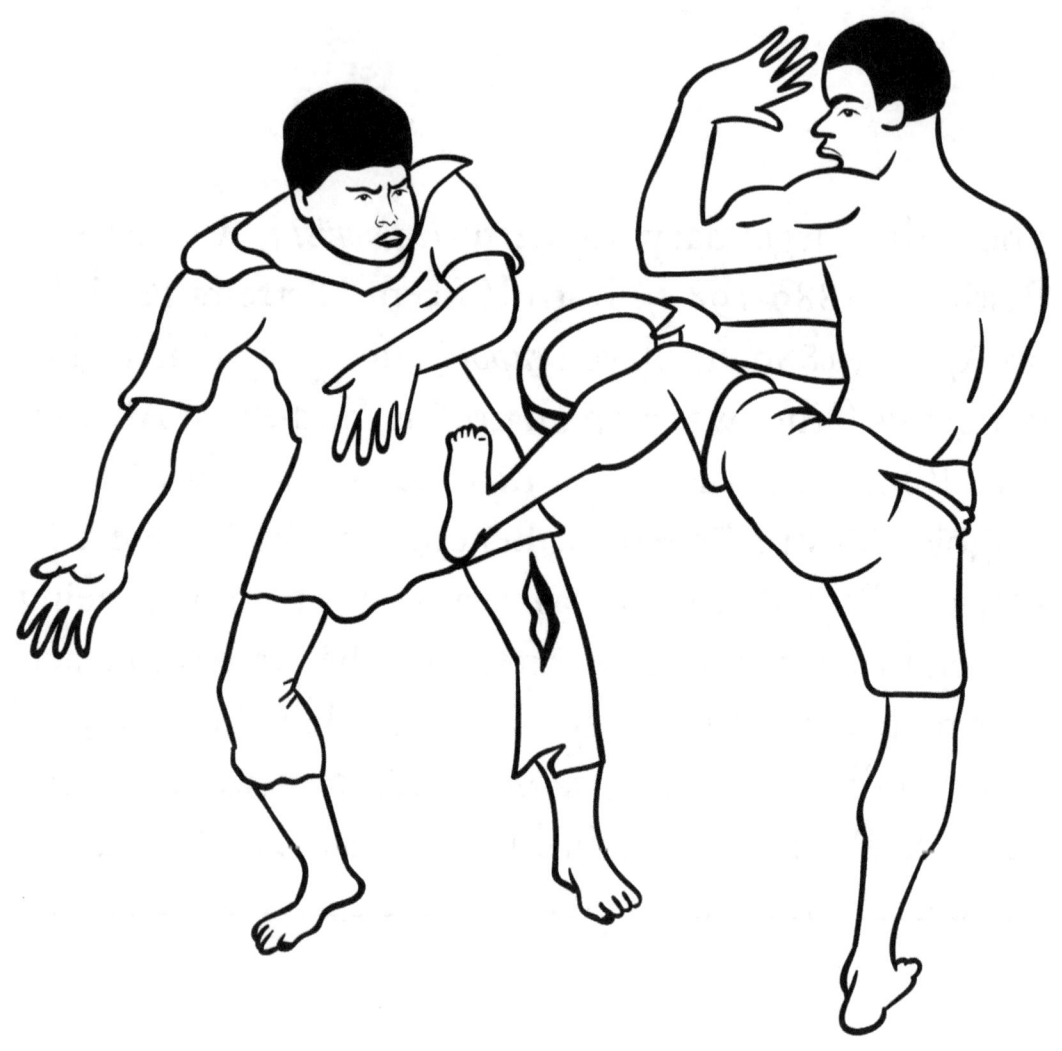

Capoeira scene in Rio de Janeiro, Brazil, 1824.

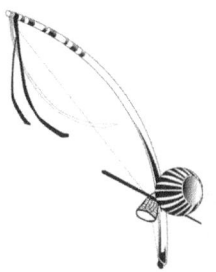

Whereas Bimba was the great innovator, Pastinha was the great traditionalist. Pastinha wanted his students to understand the practice, philosophy, and tradition of pure *capoeira angola*. As he said:

> *I practice the true capoeira angola and in my school they learn to be sincere and just. That is the Angola law. I inherited it from my grandfather. It is the law of loyalty. The capoeira angola that I learned—I did not change it here in my school. When my students go on they go on to know about everything. They know this is fight, this cunning. We must be calm. It is not an offensive fight. Capoeira waits...*

Capoeira scene in Brazil, 1830s.

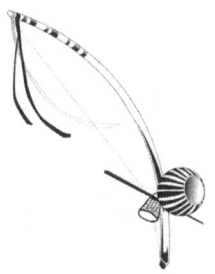

One of Pastinha's students, Mestre João Grande (João Oliveira do Santos), was born on January 15, 1933, in the tiny village of Itagi in the southern part of Bahia. His journey from the backwoods of Brazil to New York City was neither short nor easy. His birthplace is so small that it does not appear on many of the state maps.

Mestre João Grande, 1998.

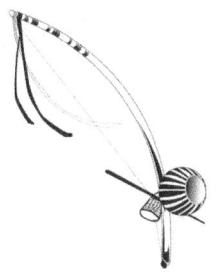

Most of Itagi's inhabitants eked out a living as farm laborers receiving subsistence wages. The family of João Grande was no different. For little João there was no time for school or even play; it was all hard work. But he lived in the countryside, so it was easy for him to engage in his favorite pastime, studying nature. He was fascinated by the movement of trees in the wind, waves in the ocean, and especially the movements of animals, like the strike of a snake and the flight of a bird. João studied them with dedication. This was to have great influence on his practice and philosophy of *capoeira*. In fact, his first and only master, Mestre Pastinha, would later give him the nickname *Gavião* (Hawk) because of the manner in which he swept down on an opponent like a bird of prey. But João's father didn't appreciate his young son's activities; he wanted him to spend more time working. It was a difficult life.

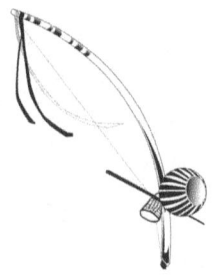

At the age of ten João saw a *capoeirista* demonstrating a movement called *corta' capim* (cut the grass). It is performed by crouching down, extending one leg, and swinging it in a rotary motion under you. Each time the swinging leg approaches the crouching leg, you hop. This allows the swinging leg to continue its circular course uninterrupted. Fascinated by the movement, he was told it was "the dance of the Nagôs," black people in the city of Salvador roughly 825 miles away, in the state of Bahia. To people of the countryside like João, all people of African descent in Salvador were Nagô or Yorùbá. But the dance was actually of Central African origin; it was *capoeira*. João didn't learn its correct name until many years later. At the age of ten he left home in search of "the dance of the Nagôs."

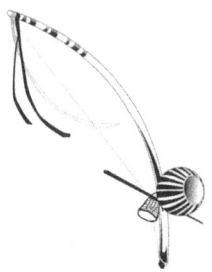

João worked and walked his way through the countryside, seeking the intriguing dance. He eked out a living on the plantations and farms of Bahia. After ten years of slow travel, he was taken to Salvador by the family with whom he was living. João was now twenty years old and in the epicenter of *capoeira,* but he didn't know what it was called or where it could be found. Each day was full of ill-paid but hard labor. One day he was sent to *Roça do Lobo* (Clearing of the Wolf), a famous site for *capoeira*. Approaching the large crowd, he could see only the tops of sticks waving in the center. It was a *capoeira roda* with the *berimbau* sticks dancing in rhythm to the music. It wasn't just a run-of-the-mill street *roda:* It was a meeting of the important *capoeira* personalities, including João Pequeno, who was there with Mestre Barboza.

Mestres João Grande, João Pequeno, and Jair Mouro.

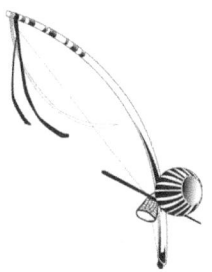

An enthralled João asked Mestre Barboza what this game was called and was told, "That is *capoeira*." João asked where he could learn it. Mestre Barboza sent him to João Pequeno, who then sent him to Mestre Pastinha. Pastinha had a famous academy in Brotas, and his *rodas* were full of the most famous names in *capoeira*. This was *capoeira* heaven. At the age of twenty, João requested permission to join Pastinha's academy.

Mestre Pastinha accepted João as a student, which had a profound effect on João. As João stated, "Pastinha was my father, my grandfather, my everything in *capoeira*." At the academy, João Pequeno, who until his death in 2011 was the oldest master still teaching, became his lifelong friend.

Musical bow of Kenya, East Africa.

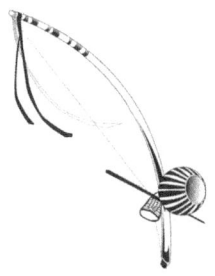

João Grande (Big John)—so called because in an inverted capoeira logic he was smaller than his friend João Pequeno (Little John)—was again studying and working. Like many other *capoeiristas,* he worked as a stevedore in Salvador's port by day. It was a back-breaking job to unload heavy sacks from the boats. An exhausted but happy João studied *capoeira* at night in Pastinha's academy. João Grande was fast becoming one of the most respected *capoeiristas* in Bahia. While still with Mester Pastinha he also studied with the great Mestre Cobrinha Verde (Rafael Alves França), who was his friend and neighbor. Few would play João in street *rodas* for fear of being publicly embarrassed.

Capoeira scene at the port of Salvador.

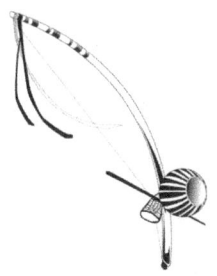

João Grande was so highly appreciated that when Carybé, a painter famous for his documentation of African culture in Bahia, wanted to do studies of *capoeira* he chose João Grande as the model. João Grande and João Pequeno also displayed their skills in numerous films, including one in which they showed the knife techniques of the art. In 1966 Pastinha took João Grande with him to demonstrate *capoeira* in Senegal at the first International Festival of Black Arts.

Mestres João Grande (right) and João Pequeno playing capoeira.

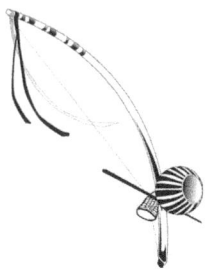

João was awarded his Diploma of *Capoeira* from Pastinha in 1968, making him a full-fledged master. In 1973 he toured Europe and the Middle East. He was now one of the symbols of *capoeira* in Bahia. In addition to playing *capoeira*, he also taught at Pastinha's academy.

Group photo of "old" capoeira mestres, 1982.

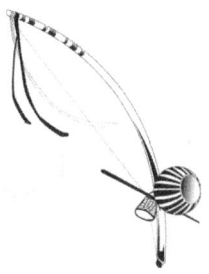

As the years passed, all did not go well at the academy. Pastinha—old, sick, and almost totally blind—was asked by the government to vacate the building in which the academy was housed. The space had been donated to Pastinha by the government, which now wanted to renovate it. Once the improvements were completed, however, the space was not returned to Pastinha. It became a training restaurant with an amphitheater and was used as a school for cooks, waiters, dancers, musicians, and others in the field. Eight years later, Pastinha died, broke and bitter about his treatment by the government, but he had never expressed regret for having lived a life of *capoeira*.

Mestre Pashinha.

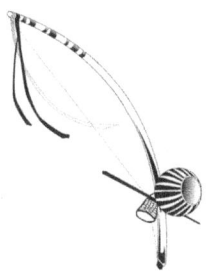

Some years later, Mestre Pastinha finally received the recognition he deserved. In a brochure celebrating his 100TH birthday, the state of Bahia declared him part of the Heritage of Bahia. Following Pastinha's death, João Grande dropped out of the *capoeira* world. He made a living working by day at a gas station and by night performing as a dancer and musician in a folkloric show for tourists. There he did not demonstrate *capoeira*. His producers wanted to see the flashy, acrobatic *capoeira regional* developed by Bimba. They didn't understand or appreciate the more complex and subtle game of *capoeira angola* played by João.

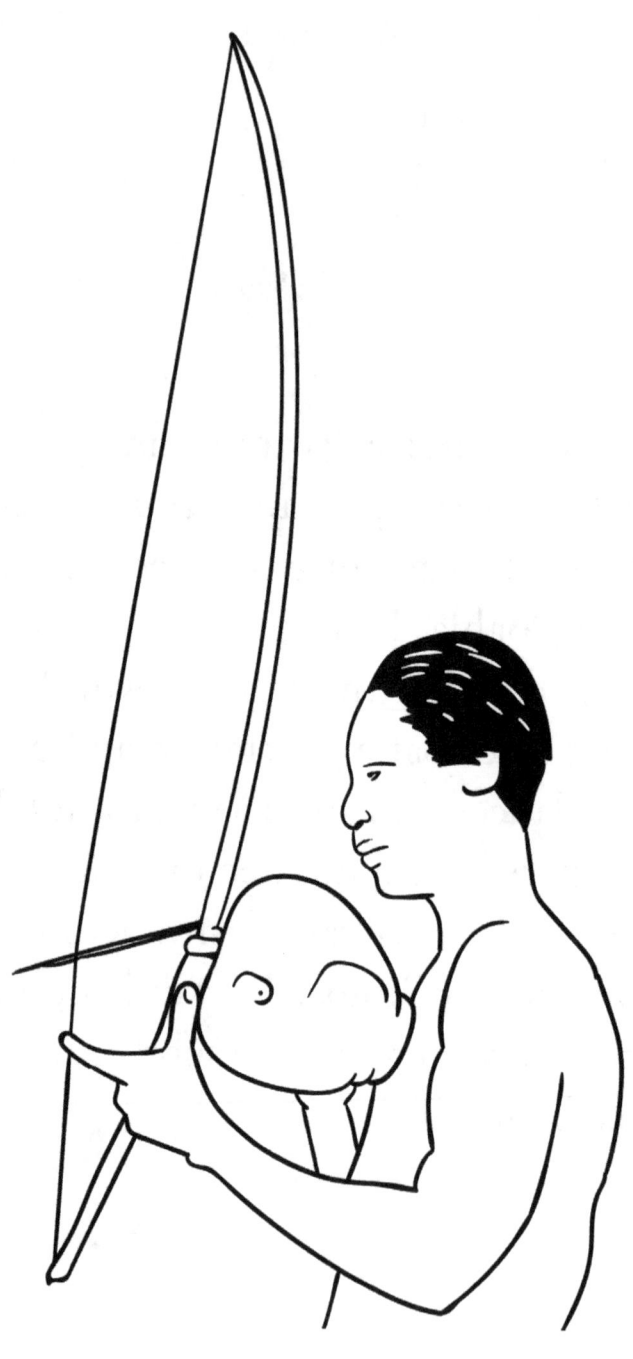

Swazi man of South Africa playing a berimbau-like instrument.

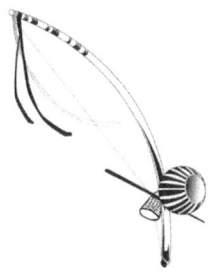

During this period, Mestre Moraes (Pedro Moraes Trinidade), who had been João Grande's prize student, returned to Bahia after almost a decade spent in Rio de Janeiro. Moraes brought with him one of his top students, Cobra Mansa (aka Cobrinha Mansa), who was now also a master. Moraes and Cobra founded Grupo de Capoeira Angola-Pelourinho (GCAP), an institution dedicated to continuing the work of Pastinha, João Grande, and the other great masters. GCAP initiated international conferences and demonstrations of *capoeira angola* and they brought together old masters to talk about the history and practice of the art. These conferences led to a revival of *capoeira angola* in Bahia. Moraes, Cobra, and GCAP wanted to educate the public about the beauty and value of African culture.

Mestre Pedro Moraes Trinidade.

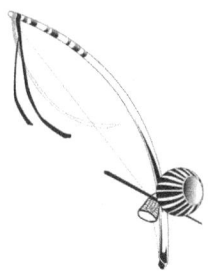

For two years Cobra and Moraes tried to persuade João Grande to return to the world of *capoeira*. Finally he agreed to join GCAP and begin teaching at their academy. After his six-year absence he was back as a teacher. Newspaper articles began to appear more frequently, and his fame and influence began to grow. In 1989 he was invited by Mestre Jelon Vieira to tour the United States to discuss and demonstrate *capoeira angola*. Fourteen years earlier Mestre Jelon had first formally introduced *capoeira regional* to the United States.

Mestres Loremil Machado, Jelon Vieira, and Bira Almeida, a student of Bimba.

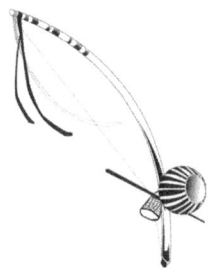

João Grande's tour was a tremendous success. In California he gave workshops for the school of Mestre Bira Almeida, a writer on *capoeira* and a student of Mestre Bimba. Practitioners of *capoeira regional* were interested in *capoeira angola*. When João Grande returned to Brazil, he was awarded the Brazilian National Sports Medal of Merit by the government. He subsequently received numerous awards and citations. In 1990 he again traveled to the United States to present *capoeira* at the National Black Arts Festival in Atlanta, Georgia. In the same year Mestres João Grande, Moraes, Cobra, Nego Gato, and Contra-Mestre Themba Mashama performed at the Schomburg Center for Research in Black Culture in New York City. They were part of an international conference, "Dancing Between Two Worlds: Kongo-Angola Culture and the Americas." Mestre Grande performed *capoeira angola* for then Mayor David Dinkins of New York City, and he began teaching an international group of students through his Capoeira Angola Center in that city.

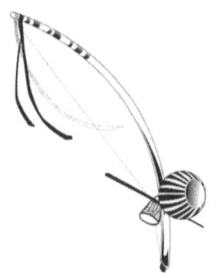

In 1995 Mestre João Grande became Dr. João Grande when he received an Honorary Doctorate of Humane Letters from Upsala University in East Orange, New Jersey. And, in September 2001 in a ceremony the White House in Washington, DC, he was awarded the National Heritage Fellowship by the National Endowment for the Arts (NEA). This award recognizes the recipient as one of the greatest living masters of an artistic tradition. This NEA Fellowship was again celebrated in July 2017 as a special activity of the 50TH Anniversary Smithsonian Folklife Festival on the Mall in Washington, DC.

João Grande receiving honorary degree from Upsala University, 1994.

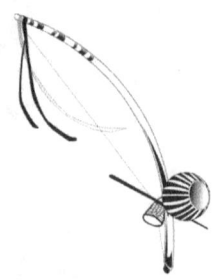

Mestre João Grande, like his teacher Mestre Pastinha, has dedicated his life to the practice and teaching of *capoeira angola*. Since the 1960s he has continuously traveled internationally to Africa, Asia, Europe and the Americas to teach about his African-based art and culture. He too has become a great philosopher of the art. In the newspaper *Portugal/Brazil,* Brazilian artist Claudia Gonçalves has written a beautiful description of João Grande:

> *For João Grande, capoeira is an exercise of the soul. Its movements inspired by nature [are] so pure that they can be recognized in any and all physical activity. Mestre João identifies these movements in all that he observes: 'A person on the bus is able to make a movement of capoeira. All that moves, man, child, cat, snake, fish, tree, always make the movement of capoeira...'*

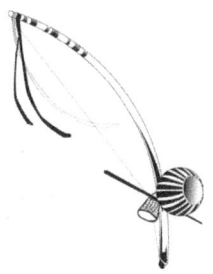

'In capoeira angola, premeditated strikes don't exist. All depends on the capoeirista. There at the moment can appear techniques never seen before. An angoleiro is never able to say that he/she has learned everything about capoeira.'

Mestres João Grande and Cobra Mansa.

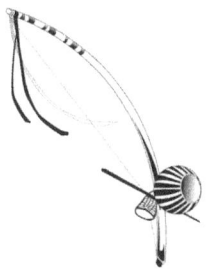

This ancient art and its masters teach one how to encounter harsh experiences while remaining flexible and receptive; how to respond to social violence with evasion and grace; and how to use the trials and tribulations of life to develop physical stamina, spiritual strength, and wisdom in one's thoughts and actions. *Capoeira angola* is ancestral wisdom passed on so that each person can make the best of their times and possibilities, creating balanced and productive lives, while adding some beauty to the world.

FURTHER READINGS

Bira Almeida, *Capoeira, a Brazilian Art Form: History, Philosophy, and Practice* (Berkeley: North Atlantic Books, 1986)

Nestor Capoeira, *The Little Capoeira Book* (Berkeley: Blue Snake Books, 2007)

T. J. Desch-Obi, *Fighting for Honor: The History of African Martial Art Traditions in the Atlantic World* (Columbia: University of South Carolina Press, 2008).

Kenneth Dossar, "Capoeira Angola: Dancing Between Two Worlds," *Afro-Hispanic Review* 11, nos. 1-3 (1992): 11-20.

Alejandro Frigerio, "Capoeira Angola: More Than a Martial Art," *Karate Kung-Fu Illustrated* 19, no. 8 (1988): 38-42.

Robert Farris Thompson, "Black Martial Arts of the Caribbean," *Review: Latin American Literature and Arts* 37 (1987): 44-47.

Printed in the USA
CPSIA information can be obtained
at www.ICGtesting.com
LVHW081457060624
782491LV00008B/1043